Authority of the King

Walking in the Way of Christ & the Apostles
Study Guide Series
Part 2, Book 7
A 6-Session Study

Peter Briggs

ISBN-13: 978-1-947642-10-2

Daystar

Published by:

Daystar Institute/NM, Inc.
P.O. Box 50567
Albuquerque, NM 87181
www.DaystarInstituteNM.us

Distributed in Africa by:

Daystar Institute / Africa
Kampala, Uganda

www.DaystarInstituteAfrica.org

Table of Contents

Table of Figures

WitW
Walking in the Way of
Christ & the Apostles

Introduction

Jesus Christ, in His three-year ministry with His twelve disciples, modeled the method for teaching disciples to walk in His way.

The Walking in the Way (WitW) Study Guide Series attempts to model Christ's method of teaching by utilizing a holistic approach designed to challenge students to apply biblical principles to their lives and ministries. Our aim is to equip disciples of Jesus to "walk in him, rooted and built up in him and established in the faith, just as you were taught, abounding in thanksgiving." Colossians 2:6,7. Thus, we emphasize wholehearted discipleship, practical Christian theology, and a biblical world view.

We have prayerfully designed the WitW study materials to equip you with the tools and concepts needed to achieve this goal. May the word of God dwell in our hearts richly through faith by studying it, reflecting upon it, and allowing it to penetrate the deepest recesses of our souls. By this means, we bring our hearts and minds into alignment with God's heart and mind.

How to Use this Study Guide

Although this Bible study may be done independently, we strongly recommend using it in a group setting. Study each session prayerfully and reflect deeply on the included passages of Scripture as part of your daily devotional time with God. Establish a journal in which you record your answers to questions, as well as your reflections and notes.

If you are participating in a group study, be prepared to interact with your leader and group members. This includes sharing insights and practical lessons God is teaching you personally. Read the questions and associated Scripture passages aloud and stick to the Bible as your sole authority for answers given. At the end of each discussion session, take time to pray for group member needs; then hold one another accountable for putting the lessons learned into practice.

Upon completion of one book, move on to the next book in the series. In parallel, begin sharing the WitW teaching with family members, work associates, and others in your circle of influence.

Leaders may use their discretion as to how much material to cover in any given discussion session. We also encourage Bible study teachers and leaders to read the associated WitW Theological Handbook or Theological Reader in order to gain a better understanding of the material presented in this booklet. Our resources are listed in the back of this study guide and are available on Amazon.com.

Introduction to Book 7

In the WitW Part 2 study guide series we discuss the first aspect of the two-part Christian gospel that was introduced in SG6 of WitW Part 1; namely, the gospel of the kingdom of God. This is the aspect of the Christian gospel that is emphasized in the Synoptic Gospels (i.e., Matthew, Mark, and Luke) and the Book of Acts. It appeals most strongly to the Jewish mind, and it confronts human prideful rebellion against the righteous rule of God.

Very few kingdoms still exist today. They have generally been replaced by democracies, republics, or dictatorships. From a human perspective and regardless of the form of government, rulers can only govern within the bounds of the authority conferred upon them through royal succession, elections, coups, or some other means. However, from a spiritual perspective, we recognize from Scripture that God in His sovereignty places individuals in positions of authority and establishes the boundaries of nations.

In general, only a fully qualified individual could aspire to be king over an earthly domain. However, in the case of the kingdom of God, that office is not subject to human appointment or general election but is in the hands of God the Father.

Jesus Christ is uniquely qualified and divinely authorized to rule over the kingdom of God.

Goals

1. To understand that God the Father has conferred absolute, sovereign authority over the entire universe upon His Son, Jesus Christ our Lord.

2. To understand that the proper response to the gospel of the kingdom of God is to repent of our prideful rebellion, submit to the kingly authority of Jesus Christ, and embrace the gospel with wholehearted trust and obedience.

Notes & Reflections

Take a moment to record your personal goals and objectives for this study of the meaning of discipleship. Also, make note of any additional insights or comments as you begin this study.

Session 1. Messiah as King

Matthew 28:18. Then Jesus came near and said to them, "All authority has been given to Me in heaven and on earth."

What an amazing statement! All authority in heaven and on earth – that is, all authority over the entire universe – had been conferred upon Jesus Christ by God the Father. In this session we discover that God the Father formally conferred upon Jesus the title King of the Universe in conjunction with Jesus' resurrection from the dead.

The prophets of the Hebrew Scriptures understood that when Messiah came, He would establish a kingdom that would encompass all nations and would be unending.

Daniel 7:13-14. I continued watching in the night visions, and I saw One like a son of man coming with the clouds of heaven. He approached the Ancient of Days and was escorted before Him. He was given authority to rule, and glory, and a kingdom; so that those of every people, nation, and language should serve Him. His dominion is an everlasting dominion that will not pass away, and His kingdom is one that will not be destroyed.

Q1. Based upon Daniel's vision, describe the nature, scope, and duration of Messiah's kingdom. Who are His subjects?

Daniel's ministry began during the early part of Nebuchadnezzar's reign (ca. 605 BC) and continued to at least the 3rd year of Cyrus the Persian (ca. 536 BC). Now fast forward 566 years to the early part of the 1st century AD.

Read Mark 15:43 and Luke 1:5, 2:25 & 2:36.

Q2. What do these four verses have in common?

Here we have four individuals, Zechariah the priest, Simeon, Anna, and Joseph of Aramathea, who were eagerly awaiting the coming of Messiah and the establishment of the kingdom of God on earth.

Confused Expectations

In our study of SG4 in WitW Part 1, we discussed examples of how the prophets of the Hebrew Scriptures all saw a single coming of Messiah; that is, the first and second advents were conflated. (See Figure 3 in Session 7 of SG4, together with the associated discussion). It would be correct for us to state that the prophets of the Hebrew Scriptures saw the two advents of Messiah according to a divine perspective rather than a human perspective. Because of this, there existed considerable confusion among Jews of the early 1st century AD as to how the kingdom of God would present itself.

Q3. What did the Jews of the early 1st century AD expect in terms what kind of leader Messiah would be and how the kingdom of God would develop?

The fact is evident that the Jews of Jesus' day expected a dynamic and magnificent appearance of the Messiah King to establish His earthly reign, which would be accompanied by the vanquishing of Israel's enemies. Israel would then be established as the preeminent nation under the kingship of the Messiah, far surpassing its greatest former glory, and the Messiah would reign forever.

Q4. Describe the religious and political conditions in Israel in the early 1st century AD. How did these conditions influence, and even shape, expectations regarding how the Messiah King would present Himself?

Life was very difficult for the average Jew living in Israel during the early part of the 1st century AD. Rome exerted brutal hegemony over the entire Mediterranean basin, including the Levant, a strip of arable land lying along the eastern shore of the Mediterranean Sea between the Euphrates River and the northeast boundary of Egypt. In encompasses the modern territories of Israel, Lebanon and the western edges of Jordan and Syria, and most particularly Israel. At the time of Jesus' birth, Herod the Great governed the entire nation in the name of the empire. After his death and during the period of Jesus' ministry, the country was divided into several governorships headed by various of Herod's relatives. The Jewish leaders, especially the priests, aligned themselves with the Roman governors in order to maintain peace and to sustain some semblance of authority.

In the religious sphere, the monotheistic character of the religion of the Jews stood in stark contrast to the polytheism of the Greeks and Romans, and, in fact, to that of all other ancient peoples and cultures. This situation was further exacerbated by the claim of the Roman emperors to be divine. As a consequence, a Jew who was intent on practicing his religion according to the law of Moses, was met with disdainful tolerance or worse on the part of the Romans.

Therefore, the coming of the Messiah, to most of the waiting Jews, was a time of consummation and fulfillment of all the glorious restoration promises of the Hebrew Scriptures.

Acts 1:6. So when they had come together, they asked Him, "Lord, are You restoring the kingdom to Israel at this time?"

Q5. What was the context of this question posed to Jesus? Who posed it and why?

Even the disciples held false expectations as to what the kingdom of God would be like after Jesus' resurrection. Consider John the Baptist's warning in the 3rd chapter of Matthew's Gospel.

Matthew 3:1 & 2. In those days John the Baptist came, preaching in the Wilderness of Judea and saying, "Repent, because the kingdom of heaven has come near!"

Q6. What was John the Baptist's principal requirement for kingdom citizenship?

John the Baptist recognized that the kingdom of heaven was at hand, and could only be entered into by a people whose lives were aligned with the ways of God. For that reason, he demanded repentance and a godly lifestyle which manifested the reality of that repentance. He rebuked the Pharisees and Sadducees for thinking they could enter the kingdom of God on the basis of religious works without understanding its spiritual and moral requirements.

John the Baptist established the principle of repentance as a requirement for kingdom citizenship.

The word "repent" translates the Greek word matanoeo, which means the act of changing one's thinking or attitude about something. Recalling our discussions in SG3, repentance is a representational act whereby a way that was previously considered acceptable and even pleasurable is now considered abhorrent. True repentance should engender a change in behavior. To feel badly and say "I'm sorry" is a good start, but unless there is a change of behavior to go along with an expression of sorrow, repentance has not occurred.

1 John 1:9. If we confess our sins, He is faithful and righteous to forgive us our sins and to cleanse us from all unrighteousness. [HCSB, emphasis added]

Confession is an act that is associated with true repentance. The Greek word which is translated "confess" in 1 John 1:9 is homologeo, which literally means to say the same thing. Like repentance, confession is a representational act whereby we agree with God in His representation of a thought, word, or action as sinful.

The essence of sin is prideful rebellion against the righteous rule of God. True repentance entails confession and brings about a turning from our way of rebellion and sin and walking in the way of God.

Q7. Based upon the record of his ministry in the four Gospels, when and in what form did John the Baptist expect the kingdom of God to present itself?

Unlike Daniel, John the Baptist was not looking toward a far-term fulfillment of prophecy, but rather a near-term one. "The kingdom of heaven is at hand," he proclaimed, and that kingdom would soon be ushered in by Jesus Christ Himself. John embraced the fact that he was the Messenger prophesied in the 3rd chapter of Malachi whose ministry was to prepare the people of Israel to receive their Messiah. John did not regard kingdom citizenship as universal; instead it was reserved for those who experienced genuine repentance, and who turned from their sinful ways and walked in the way of Yahweh. This was not at all what the religious leaders of the day expected. With his emphasis on repentance, John prepared the way for a new kingdom paradigm.

The kingdom of God would first of all be spiritual and moral, rather than geographical and political.

A New Kingdom Paradigm

A paradigm is a way of looking at something. As we mentioned earlier, the Jews of Jesus' day were looking for a geographical and political kingdom – one that would restore Israel to her former glory and free them from bondage to Rome. That was their kingdom paradigm.

Read the Sermon on the Mount (Matthew 5:1 – 7:29), the Great Commission (Matthew 28:18-20), Luke 17:20-21, and John 3:1-5.

Q8. Based upon the passages listed above, describe Jesus' kingdom paradigm.

From the beginning of His ministry, Christ repeatedly announced His intention to establish the kingdom of God. The Sermon on the Mount is essentially His enumeration of the qualifications and requirements for kingdom citizenship. Only the King Himself, or His ambassador, would possess the authority to proclaim the laws of the kingdom. It is impossible to miss the close connection in the Sermon on the Mount between kingdom citizenship and righteousness, such as clearly stated by Jesus in the following passage from the 5th chapter of Matthew:

Matthew 5:19-20. Therefore, whoever deprives of its authority one of the least of these commands and teaches people to do the same will be called least in the kingdom of heaven. But whoever practices and teaches these commands will be called great in the kingdom of heaven. For I tell you, unless your righteousness surpasses that of the scribes and Pharisees, you will never enter the kingdom of heaven. [Adapted from the HCSB]

Q9. According to this passage, what is the primary qualification for becoming a citizen of the kingdom of heaven? Is this standard humanly attainable? Why or why not?

Q10. Based upon your studies thus far, how would you define righteousness?

We will unpack the meaning of righteousness later, but suffice it say that our understanding of righteousness begins with the character of God, whose moral uprightness and justice are absolute. Moreover, He personifies absolute truth and holiness, and He always acts with abundant grace, mercy, and compassion. This is the kind of righteousness that is spoken of by the Apostle Paul in the following passage from the 3rd chapter of Philippians:

Philippians 3:8-9. Because of the supreme advantage of knowing Christ Jesus my Lord, I count everything else as loss. In fact, for Him I have accepted the loss of all other things and look on them all as refuse if only I can gain Christ and be given a place in Him, not having my own righteousness that comes from the law, but that which comes from the faith of Christ – the righteousness from God that depends on faith. [Adapted from the HCSB]

When a person wholeheartedly embraces the Christian gospel, he receives the imputed righteousness of Christ as a gift. This is the only way that our righteousness before God can exceed that of the scribes and Pharisees in accordance with the passage quoted above from the 5th chapter of Matthew.

Matthew 12:28. If I drive out demons by the Spirit of God, then the kingdom of God has come upon you. [Adapted from HCSB]

Q11. In this passage, what was Jesus claiming about the scope and presence of the kingdom of God in relation to Himself?

During Jesus' earthly ministry, when he was healing the sick and casting out demons, thereby demonstrating the power of God to the astonished crowds, he was effectively proclaiming that the promised Messianic kingdom was, in fact, breaking into their reality, as seen in the verse quoted above.

Importance of Acknowledging the King

Another radical element of the kingdom teaching of Christ is His assertion that the kingdom of God had already existed and had belonged to the nation of Israel. Yet their refusal to abide by the laws of the kingdom, and their rejection of the authority of God as their King were grounds for the kingdom of God being wrested from their grasp. Therefore, to be a part of His kingdom today, it is imperative that we acknowledge and submit to the authority of the King, who is, in fact, Jesus Christ, the promised Messiah.

Read Isaiah 5:1-7 and Matthew 8:10-12 & 21:43.

Q12. Based upon these passages from Isaiah's prophecy and Matthew's Gospel, summarize how Isaiah and Jesus represented the fact that the kingdom of God had belonged to Israel, but now was being taken from them?

Q13. How do Isaiah and Jesus represent the fact that the Jewish people had disqualified themselves from being citizens of the kingdom of God? What, specifically, had they done, or failed to do, which brought about their disqualification?

It is impossible to take something away from someone who never possessed it in the first place. Therefore, the implication is that the people had disqualified themselves from being kingdom citizens because they failed to produce kingdom fruits. The manner in which we live our lives is crucial to authenticating our belief and right to claim kingdom citizenship.

Jesus, Son of Man

As you scan through the gospels, you will quickly notice that one of Jesus' favorite terms in representing Himself is the title Son of man. Thus Daniel, in using the term "son of man" in Daniel 7:13, was actually referring to Christ as King. The Hebrew prophets understood that when Messiah came, He would establish a kingdom that would never pass away or be destroyed. Its citizens would be people from every tribe and language, gathered to serve their Messiah King. In fact, Daniel 9:25-27 even predicted exactly when Messiah would come.

As the years rolled by from the time of Daniel, the Jews groaned under the tyranny of foreign rulers. Generation after generation of devout Jews longed for the coming of the promised Messiah. They were convinced from their Scriptures that He would break the yoke of tyranny and bondage from off their necks, establish Israel as the head of the nations, and rule over the entire world from the throne of King David in Jerusalem.

Restoration Promises

It is no wonder there was such confusion among Jews of the early 1st century AD in view of their understanding of what the kingdom of God was to be like from the prophecies of the Hebrew Scriptures. Consider the following promise in the 30th chapter of Jeremiah:

Jeremiah 30:3. ... "For the days are certainly coming" – this is Yahweh's declaration – "when I will restore the fortunes of My people Israel and Judah... and I will restore them to the land I gave to their ancestors and they will possess it."

They expected a political and geographic kingdom, where Israel would be the foremost of all nations, surpassing its greatest former glory. Their Messiah King would reign over the entire world from the throne of His forefather, King David. He would save them from Roman oppression, and He would restore Israel's national identity. His kingdom would endure forever and ever. To most of the waiting Jews, this was the consummation of all the glorious restoration promises of the Hebrew Scriptures.

Moral and Spiritual Kingdom

However, the new kingdom paradigm introduced by John the Baptist and proclaimed by Jesus Christ was not a geographical and political kingdom, but rather a moral and spiritual one where righteousness ruled. Its laws were based upon the Ten Commandments and the Sermon on the Mount, which not only demanded an outward display of morality, but one that sprang from the very heart of man. Unbelief and the refusal of the people of Israel to abide by the laws of the kingdom, and their rejection of the authority of God as their King were grounds for their being rejected from the kingdom of God. Therefore, to be a part of His kingdom today, we must repent of our prideful rebellion against His righteous rule and submit to Jesus Christ as our Messiah King. The domain over which He rules includes all of heaven and all of earth, and the duration of His kingdom is forever and ever.

Kingdom citizens are those who have repented of their prideful rebellion, received by faith the salvation that Jesus Christ, the Son of

God, procured for us at such a horrendous cost, submitted to his righteous rule, and are now walking in His way.

Q14. Given the glory, majesty, extent, and duration of the kingdom of God, reflect on how you, as a kingdom citizen, are displaying character qualities required by the King, and exemplified by Him during His life and ministry.

Notes & Reflections

Session 2. Establishment of Christ's Kingly Authority

Was Jesus' authority as the Messiah or Christ ever clearly affirmed? Scripture goes to great lengths to establish this point, so that we would have no doubt as to whom we owe our allegiance as subjects. There are only two possible responses: either we serve the Lord with reverence, joy, and love and receive the accompanying blessing for all those who take refuge in Him; or we continue in our prideful rebellion and autonomy, and we perish in the way.

Read Psalm 2.

The 2nd Psalm is a coronation psalm, majestic in its declaration that the King who is seated on the throne of God's kingdom would reign forever and over the entire earth.

Q1. Based upon your analysis of the 2nd Psalm, what parts of this Psalm support the claim that it is a coronation psalm?

A coronation proclamation is found in the 7th verse:

Psalm 2:7. I will declare Yahweh's decree: He said to Me, "You are My Son; today I have become Your Father." [Adapted from the HCSB]

The church fathers regarded Psalm 2:7 as a prophetical reference to Christ's incarnation[1]. However, the result of more recent research concludes that the "today" event of Psalm 2:7 corresponds, in fact, to the Messianic King's

---

[1] Refer to Oden, Gen. Ed., (2006), New Testament Volume V, pp. 164-167.

accession to the throne rather than His birth[2]. In this connection, the kings of ancient Israel were regarded as becoming the sons of God in conjunction with their coronation rather than their birth. This interpretation is borne out by John Calvin in his commentary on the Book of Acts. Consider the following two passages from Matthew's Gospel that record God the Father formally conferring the title "Son" on Jesus of Nazareth:

Matthew 3:17. And there came a voice from heaven: This is My beloved Son. I take delight in Him!

Matthew 17:5. While he was still speaking, suddenly a bright cloud covered them, and a voice from the cloud said: This is My beloved Son. I take delight in Him. Listen to Him!

Q2. From the two passages quoted above, on what two significant occasions did God formally confer the title of "Son" on Jesus of Nazareth?

The title of Son was confirmed by God the Father at Jesus Christ baptism and again at the transfiguration event. God the Father proclaimed Jesus Christ as His Son three crucial times: at His baptism, His transfiguration, and His resurrection. This strong affirmation is aligned with the trilogy of words for emphasis as in Holy, Holy, Holy!

Read Acts 13:13-41.

This passage records the ministry of Paul and Barnabas at Pisidian Antioch. The 33rd verse is especially noteworthy:

Acts 13:33. God has fulfilled this for us, their children, by raising up Jesus, as it is written in the second Psalm: You are My Son; today I have become Your Father.

---

[2] Refer to Keil & Kelitzsch (2001), vol.5, p. 53.

Q3. What is the connection between Psalm 2:7 and Acts 13:33?

Did you notice that Paul is making a direct connection between the "today" event of Psalm 2:7 to the resurrection event of Acts 13:33? In other words, Jesus' kingship was formally and firmly established in connection with His resurrection, for it was then that he ascended into heaven to assume His place reigning at the right hand of God.

Read Psalm 24.

The 24th Psalm is a coronation song celebrating the Son's accession to the throne of the universe.

Q4. Which parts of Psalm 24 confirm that it is indeed a coronation psalm?

David proclaims the majestic entrance of the Messianic King through the gates of heaven as the newly crowned King of glory. Imagine yourself standing in awe at the gates of heaven as the victorious King of glory enters.

Romans 1:4. ... And who has been declared to be the powerful Son of God by the resurrection from the dead according to the Spirit of holiness.

Q5. What confirmation do you find in Romans 1:4 of Christ's resurrection being crucial to his being crowned King?

Paul affirms that Jesus Christ was declared to be the Son of God in power according to the Spirit of holiness by his resurrection from the dead.

1 Corinthians 15:27. For God has put everything under His feet. But when it says "everything" is put under Him, it is obvious that He who puts everything under Him is the exception.

Q6. Analyze the significance of this verse in the context of the 15th chapter of 1 Corinthians with regard to Christ's universal kingly authority.

Read Philippians 2:5-11.

Q7. Identify the characteristics of King Jesus, and His desired response from us.

On account of Jesus' supreme act of self-emptying, God the Father has exalted Him to the highest place and rank, and He has conferred upon Him the Name which is above every name, that at the name of Jesus every knee should bow. Thus, we can state with confidence that God the Father formally bestowed upon His Son kingly authority over the cosmos in conjunction with His resurrection.

Q8. How well do you think our Easter celebrations reflect the celebration of Jesus' coronation when he officially became the King of glory? Explain your answer.

The coronation event that established Christ on His throne at the Father's right hand as the King of the universe took place in conjunction with His resurrection.

The Name That Is Above Every Name

In the 1st and 2nd chapters of Genesis, the writer introduces two names of God – Elohim and Yahweh. Elohim is an appellative divine name – that is, a title – and Yahweh is God's personal or proper name. Elohim signifies God's transcendence – the fact that He resides far above us in the heavens. Yahweh, on the other hand, signifies God's immanence, the fact that He is relationally near to His people; in particular, He is intimately aware of our needs and eager to meet them.

Throughout the Septuagint (the Greek translation of the Hebrew Scriptures), the Greek word Kyrios is used to translate God's personal name, Yahweh. Kyrios is the literal equivalent of the English "lord" or "master." This probably explains why modern English translations of the Hebrew Scriptures employ "Lord" to represent Yahweh. Since the Septuagint was the translation of the Hebrew Scriptures used by Jesus and the apostles, they also commonly employed Kyrios to represent Yahweh.

In fact, in every case where Christ or the apostles quoted a passage from the Hebrew Scriptures containing God's personal name, they used Kyrios to represent Yahweh.

Philippians 2:9-11. For this reason God highly exalted Him and gave Him the name that is above every name, so that at the name of Jesus every knee will bow – of those who are in heaven and on earth and under the earth – and every tongue should confess that Jesus Christ is Lord (= Kyrios), to the glory of God the Father.

John 8:58. Jesus said to them, "I assure you: Before Abraham was, I am."

Exodus 3:14-15. Elohim replied to Moses, "I AM WHO I AM. This is what you are to say to the Israelites: I AM has sent me to you." Elohim also said to Moses, "Say this to the Israelites: Yahweh, the Elohim of your fathers, the Elohim of Abraham, the Elohim of Isaac, and the Elohim of Jacob, has sent me to you. This is My name forever; this is how I am to be remembered in every generation. [Adapted from the HCSB]

Q9. Carefully analyze these verses. Based upon your analysis, what is the name that is above every other name?

Jesus used exactly the same construction in John 8:58 as God used when revealing His name to Moses in Exodus 3:14. In this passage, "I AM WHO I AM" translates the single Hebrew word "hayah", which signifies God's absolute being or self-existence. He is dependent upon nothing or no one, but everything in His creation is dependent upon Him. In the Septuagint, "hayah" is translated as ego "eimi". If Jesus uttered the statement recorded in John 8:58 in the Greek language, He employed "ego eimi," or, if He uttered it in Hebrew, He employed "hayah." In either case, the Jewish leaders clearly recognized what He was claiming, and they took up stones to throw at Him, because they believed He was guilty of blasphemy.

In the conversation recorded by John in the 8th chapter of his Gospel, Jesus clearly and unreservedly claims to be Yahweh, our self-existent God – the great I AM.

Read the 1st chapter of Hebrews and Romans 1:1-5.

Following are two key verses from the 1st chapter of Hebrews:

Hebrews 1:4 & 8. So He became higher in rank than the angels, just as the name He inherited is superior to theirs... But to the Son: Your throne, God, is forever and ever, and the scepter of Your kingdom is a scepter of justice.

Q10. What do these verses teach us about Jesus' kingly position and reign?

Through the window of Scripture passages like the above, we worshipfully gaze upon Jesus Christ, who is seated at the Father's right hand, having inherited the greatest name of all; He is the one and only Son of God. It is through His glorious resurrection from the dead that He inherited the fulfillment of the decree of Psalm 2:7: "You are My Son; today I have become Your Father."

In His capacity as Son of God, He reigns eternally over God's kingdom as Paul states in the following passage from the 1st chapter of Ephesians:

Ephesians 1:20-23. He demonstrated this power in the Messiah by raising Him from the dead and seating Him at His right hand in the heavens – far above every ruler and authority, power and dominion, and every title given, not only in this age but also in the one to come. And He put everything under His feet and appointed Him as head over everything for the church, which is His body, the fullness of the One who fills all things in every way.

Q11. What important facts does this passage teach us about King Jesus?

Through the Scripture passages we have studied in this session, we have learned much about Jesus' identity: the resurrected Jesus – King Jesus – is Yahweh, the Son of God, the Ancient of Days. He is superior to every agency in heaven and on earth, including the entire angelic host and the "the spiritual forces of evil in the heavens" addressed in Ephesians 6:12.

Jesus Christ is the eternal King of glory, seated at the Father's right hand, having all authority to sovereignly rule in heaven and on earth.

Jesus' authority to reign was conferred by God Himself in accordance with Psalm 2:7, confirmed at His baptism and transfiguration, and consummated in His resurrection, in conjunction with which His formal coronation ceremony was held. He now reigns as the King of glory, and He carries the name Yahweh, the relational, self-existent God – the great I AM!

Notes & Reflections

As you consider Jesus, the reigning King of the universe, bow down before Him and offer to Him your sacrifice of praise.

Ponder the significance of your being able to personally worship and have relationship with the King of the Universe. How should this impact the way you live, conduct your ministry, and relate to family, friends, and neighbors?

How would you make the argument for Jesus' sovereign authority to a person who has not yet come to faith?

Session 3. Manifestation of Christ's Kingly Authority

The Fact of Christ's Resurrection

The fact of Christ's resurrection is the clearest manifestation of His kingly authority. Is there a greater or more powerful enemy arrayed against mankind than death? Death is the implacable foe of man that stalks and eventually conquers each and every one of us. And no one has conquered death except Jesus Christ!

1 Corinthians 15:54-57.   When this corruptible is clothed with incorruptibility, and this mortal is clothed with immortality, then the saying that is written will take place: Death has been swallowed up in victory. Death, where is your victory? Death, where is your sting? Now the sting of death is sin, and the power of sin is the law. But thanks be to God, who gives us the victory through our Lord Jesus Christ!

Q1. Why is Christ's resurrection the single greatest manifestation of His kingly authority?

Read the 28th chapter of Matthew, the 16th chapter of Mark, the 24th chapter of Luke, the 20th and 21st chapters of John, and the 15th chapter of 1 Corinthians.

Q2. What evidence of the historical factuality of Christ's resurrection are recorded in these passages? What is your assessment of the strength of this documentary evidence of Christ's resurrection?

It is true that Jesus manifested His kingly authority to His followers during His life and ministry, including over the forces of nature, Satan and his demons, human illness, and even over death. However, it was only after His death and resurrection, with Him now seated at the right hand of God the Father, that His kingly authority has been placed in evidence to all mankind. Consider the events recorded by Luke in the book of Acts, including the rapid growth of the church through the ministries of the Apostle Peter and then the Apostle Paul. And now, over the course of nearly two millennia of history, Christ is bringing His kingdom into being in the face of the concerted and persistent actions of His enemies.

John Piper treats Christ's kingly authority in the 35th chapter of *Taste and See*. That chapter is entitled They Gave It Their Best Shot, referring to the efforts made by the enemies of Christ to seal Him in the tomb. However, when He was ready, He burst forth, in spite of the heavy stone that sealed the entrance and the armed guards that were posted outside. And He has been bursting forth on the world's scene ever since, such as manifested by the burgeoning growth of the Christian church in South Asia at the present time. (Refer to Piper (1999), pp. 112-113)

Read Acts 5:33-42.

Q3. How did Gamaliel's wise counsel to the Sanhedrin change the outcome of the Sanhedrin's decision? In what way does his counsel provide a lens to assess the significance of the history of the church?

Gamaliel counseled that the Sanhedrin should avoid violent action against the apostles, for, if this movement was of God, there would be nothing they could do to stop it. However, if it was merely of human origin, then it would die away of its own accord.

Needless to say, Luke's narrative in Acts in conjunction with nearly two millennia of history demonstrate which of these two options is true, thereby manifesting Christ's kingly authority to bring into being His kingdom in the face of sustained and intense opposition from the world powers of this darkness, the spiritual forces of evil in the heavens (Ephesians 6:12).

Notes & Reflections

Session 4. Application of Christ's Kingly Authority

The Great Commission

Christ's Great Commission, as recorded in the 28th chapter of Matthew's Gospel, sets forth His mandate of how His kingdom would be expanded to encompass all people groups through the making of disciples – that is, people who would become fully devoted followers of Him, and who would, in turn, share their faith with others.

Matthew 28:16-20. The 11 disciples traveled to Galilee, to the mountain where Jesus had directed them. When they saw Him, they worshiped, but some doubted. Then Jesus came near and said to them, "All authority has been given to Me in heaven and on earth. Therefore, in the process of going about your life, make disciples of all people groups, baptizing them into the name of the Father and of the Son and of the Holy Spirit, teaching them to obey everything I have commanded you. And remember, I am with you always, to the end of the age." [Adapted from the HCSB, emphasis added]

I need to offer some explanation of this important passage. In the original Greek expression, there is a single principal verb, "matheteuo", which is translated "make disciples." This verb is qualified and conditioned by three participial phrases, of which the first is customarily translated as "go." Since it is actually a participle, I have rendered it above as "in the process of going about your life." The second participial phrase begins with "baptizing," and the third begins with "teaching."

Focusing upon the second participial phrase, it is customarily rendered as "baptizing them in the name..." However, the Greek word translated "in" is actually "eis", which should be translated "into." The third participial phrase is noteworthy because the Greek word which is translated as "obey" or "observe" is "tereo", which means to guard by keeping the eyes upon. Thus, the kind of obedience to Jesus' commands which we are to teach as we make disciples is not a dutiful, external obedience, but instead it is an obedience that springs from a heart attitude of counting Jesus' commands as precious and even delightful. This is exactly the heart attitude that is reflected in the language of the 19th Psalm regarding the "instruction of Yahweh."

Q1. What was the extent and basis of Christ's kingly authority according to the Great Commission?

Because Jesus Christ was given authority over the universe by dint of his resurrection, he alone is its supreme ruler.

Q2. What is Christ's purpose in proclaiming the Great Commission, and how was it to be carried out?

Jesus commands His disciples to expand His kingdom by making more disciples. This disciple-making project would entail proclaiming the gospel, baptizing, and teaching. The command came from Christ's supreme authority as King of the universe, and it therefore not only compelled the eleven disciples to boldly move out in obedience, but it also guaranteed the ultimate success of their mission. The King who commissioned them had absolute authority on earth and in heaven, and He promised to be with them until the end of the age. Thus, as the disciples moved out in obedience, they did so as ambassadors of the King, with His full delegated authority conferred upon them. Based upon His promise, they could go forth with courage and confidence.

We also are recipients of this commission, and it is still backed up by the same weight of Christ's sovereign kingly authority together with His promise of being with us until the disciple-making project is completed.

Knowing the King and the extent of His authority is what empowers the church to continue to make disciples.

Q3. Based upon the wording of the Great Commission, describe the essence of disciple-making.

The objective of disciple-making is to bring another person under Christ's loving and merciful authority as a fully devoted follower.

Q4. What new insights have you gained from thinking about the Great Commission in the light of the authority of Jesus Christ as the King over the entire cosmos?

Q5. How will these insights affect your approach to evangelism and making disciples?

Kingdom Expansion

Kingdom expansion demands commitment and strategy. Figure 1 depicts kingdom expansion as recorded by Luke in the Book of Acts. Consider the outline for kingdom expansion asserted by Jesus in the following passage in the 1st chapter of Acts:

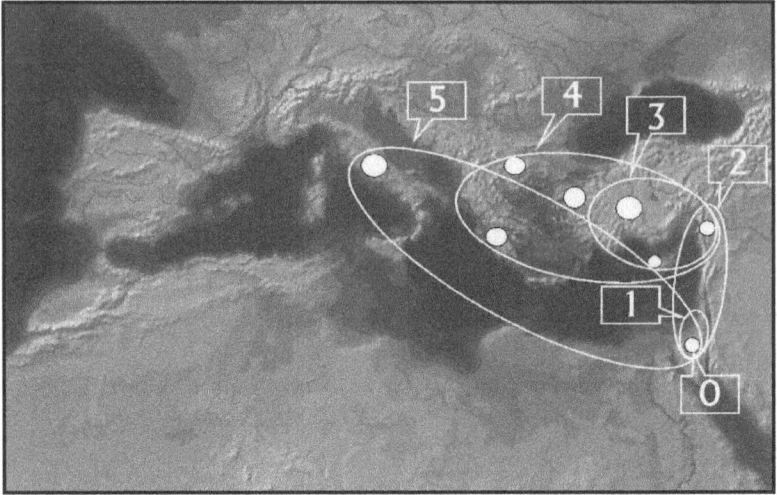

FIGURE 1. SUCCESSIVE WAVES OF KINGDOM EXPANSION

Acts 1:6-8. So when they had come together, they asked Him, "Lord, are You restoring the kingdom to Israel at this time?" He said to them, "It is not for you to know times or periods that the Father has set by His own authority. But you will receive power when the Holy Spirit has come on you, and you will be My witnesses in Jerusalem, in all Judea and Samaria, and to the ends of the earth."

Careful reading of Luke's narrative in the Book of Acts reveals five literary markers which divide the narrative into six sections, each of which describes a phase in the expansion of Christ's kingdom. As stated in the passage quoted above, the project would begin with the establishment of the church community in Jerusalem, which was the epicenter for the entire movement. The first of the literary markers is found in the 6th chapter as follows:

Acts 6:7. So the preaching about God flourished, the number of the disciples in Jerusalem multiplied greatly, and a large group of priests became obedient to the faith.

This passage exemplifies the formulation of all Luke's literary markers, which are shown in bold font in Table 1. The six phases in Table 1 correspond to the six ellipses in Figure 1.

Phase	Region	Passage
0	Jerusalem, the epicenter	Acts 1:1 - :7
1	Judea & Samaria	Acts 6:8 – 9:31
2	Syrian Antioch	Acts 9:32 – 12:24
3	Cyprus, Pamphylia & Southern Galatia	Acts 12:25 – 16:5
4	Macedonia, Achaia & Asia	Acts 16:6 – 19:20
5	Rome	Acts 19:21 – 28:31

FIGURE 2. THE SIX PHASES OF KINGDOM EXPANSION

Read each of the six sections in the Book of Acts identified above.

Q6. For each phase of kingdom expansion defined in Table 1 and delineated in Figure 1, identify the principal actor whose ministry is featured in that phase, and summarize the expansion of Christ's kingdom that took place.

The proclamation of the Christian gospel was initiated by the Apostle Peter in Jerusalem during the festival of Pentecost. Philip the Evangelist – one of the seven deacons whose commissioning is recorded in the 6th chapter of Acts – was instrumental in proclaiming the gospel in Judea and Samaria. Beginning in the third phase of kingdom expansion, the Apostle Paul becomes the principal actor. He was commissioned by Christ to proclaim the gospel to the Gentiles as indicated by Acts 9:15. He helped establish the Gentile church in Syrian Antioch, which become the sending church for his three missionary expeditions that are recorded in the Book of Acts.

The Apostle Paul was instrumental in defining the method by which the Great Commission would be fulfilled throughout the world of the Gentiles. The Pauling method begins with evangelization of a strategic metropolitan center.

Q7. What biblical principles from the Book of Acts should govern the disciple-making project commanded by Jesus Christ in the Great Commission?

Q8. What was especially significant about the church in Syrian Antioch?

The church in Syrian Antioch serves as a model for kingdom expansion in the role of sending church for the Apostle Paul and his missionary team. The regions impacted by Paul's ministry are identified in Table 1 and graphically delineated in Figure 1. The church community in Syrian Antioch exemplifies and embodies an important concept which I designate as **an Antiochean community**. The distinctive feature of an Antiochean community is that its leaders are proactive in the implementation of the disciple-making project by planting churches in their neighboring cities, towns, and villages.

Paul's Strategy for Kingdom Expansion

As stated above, Luke's narrative in the Book of Acts places in evidence the method pioneered by the Apostle Paul for implementing the Great Commission and expanding Christ's kingdom throughout the world of the Gentiles. The Pauline method consists of the following five essential phases:

- Evangelize a strategic metropolitan center.

- Gather new disciples into a church community.

- Establish the disciples in the way of Christ and the apostles.

- Order the community by appointing spiritually and morally qualified leaders to govern it.

- Charge the leaders to reproduce like established and like ordered Christian communities in neighboring cities, towns and villages.

An Antiochean community is one whose leaders actually take seriously and implement the fifth phase of the Pauline method.

Antiochean Church Communities

The prototypical Antiochean community was the church of Syrian Antioch, which served as the sending church for the Apostle Paul and his team over the course of three missionary expeditions. I believe we can safely assume that Paul intended that each of the churches to which his epistles are addressed would serve as Antiochean communities for their regions as follows:

- **Galatians**. This letter was addressed to church communities established by Paul and Barnabas during Paul's first missionary expedition. They were located in Pisidian Antioch, Iconium, Lystra, and Derbe – all of which are located in the southern region of the province of Galatia. From Luke's statement in Acts 13:49, it appears that the church in Pisidian Antioch fulfilled the role of an Antiochean community.

- **Philippians and Thessalonians**. The first church to be planted by Paul and his team in the continent of Europe was the one at Philippi. This was followed by Thessalonica. Both churches served as Antiochean communities for the expansion of the kingdom throughout the province of Macedonia.

- **Corinthians**. The church at Corinth was established by Paul and his team as part of the second missionary expedition after their ministry in Macedonia. This church served as an Antiochean community for the expansion of the kingdom throughout the province of Achaia.

- **Ephesians and Colossians**. Both Ephesus and Colossae are located in the province of Asia. The church community at Ephesus was established by Paul and his team as part of the second missionary expedition and after their ministries in Macedonia and Achaia. The church at Colossae was effectively a daughter church of the Ephesian community.

The Church at Ephesus

The establishment of the church at Ephesus is recorded in the 19th chapter of the Book of Acts.

Read Acts 19:1-41.

The 10th verse, which describes Paul's extended ministry in Ephesus, is especially noteworthy:

Acts 19:10. And this went on for two years, so that all the inhabitants of Asia, both Jews and Greeks, heard the message about the Lord.

Q9. What insights are gained from this passage regarding Paul's strategy for establishing church communities?

In the last decade of the 1 st century AD, John is the last surviving apostle. Prior to being arrested by the Roman authorities and exiled to the island of Patmos, he was ministering at Ephesus, and he was endeavoring to strengthen the church in that city as well as those in the neighboring cities in the province of Asia. After his exile, he addressed Revelation to the seven churches in Asia, beginning with Ephesus.

Read the 2nd and 3rd chapters of Revelation. 9.

Q10. List the names of the seven churches in this passage and identify their locations on the map of Figure 2.

It is highly likely that the six churches listed after Ephesus were actually daughter churches of the Ephesian church. This illustrates the value of Paul's strategy, which we outlined at the beginning of this section. Under the Holy Spirit's leadership and with His enablement, Paul targeted strategically located metropolitan centers, from which the gospel could be proclaimed and churches established in neighboring cities, towns, and villages.

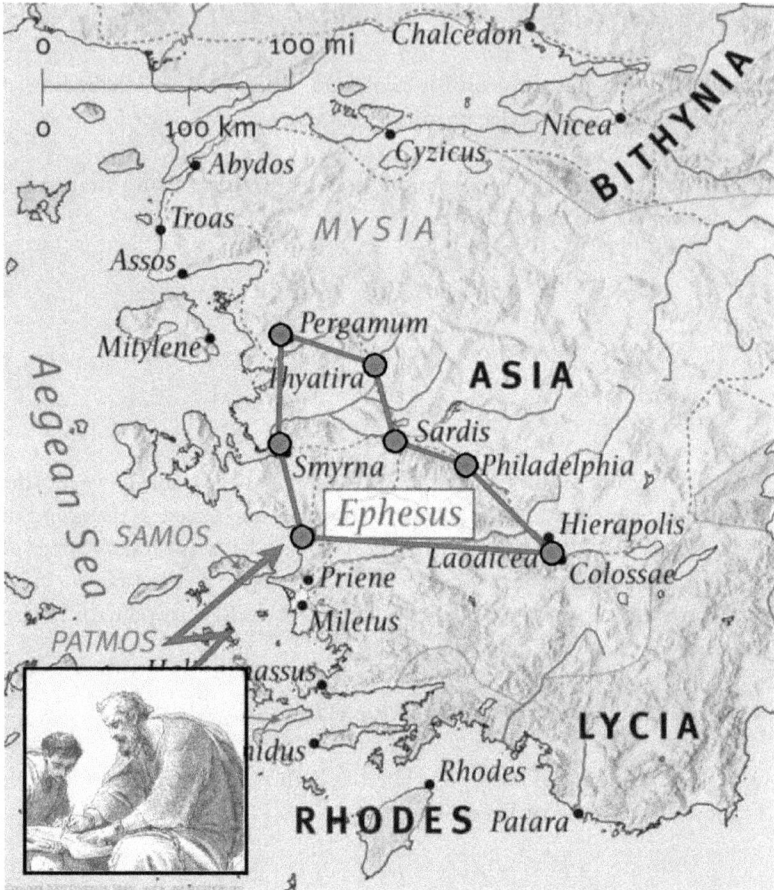

FIGURE 3. KINGDOM EXPANSION THROUGHOUT ASIA

Q11. Is Paul's strategy valid today? How can the Pauline method for kingdom expansion be practiced in your area?

Governing Principles

As we move with Paul through his three missionary expeditions, as recorded by Luke in the Book of Acts, we cannot help but be impressed Session 4. Application of Christ's Kingly Authority Page 38 with his concern for thoroughly establishing new disciples and church communities in the way of Christ and the apostles. Let me propose that we can distill Paul's concern for the churches down to three essential governing principles, which are represented by three key Greek words as follows:

- **Koinonia**. This word is often translated as "fellowship," but it actually means to have things in common, or to work together in a spirit of partnership.

- **Philadelphia**. This word can be translated as "brotherly kindness." If we are governed by a spirit of philadelphia, then we are able to put up with the foibles and idiosyncrasies of one another, and we are quick to extend forgiveness in the case of offenses.

- **Agape.** This word can be translated as unconditional, self-sacrificing love. It is the kind of love that Jesus commanded His disciples to practice with respect to one another. The 13th chapter of 1 Corinthians presents a beautiful portrait of agape and how it works out in the life of a mature disciple. Agape in combination with koinonia brings about a spirit of compassion for brothers and sisters in Christ who are in material need. This, in turn, causes Christ followers to be generous with their material assets in meeting the needs of others.

With these governing principles in place in the churches, they would clearly display to a watching world the presence of Christ among His people.

King Jesus has commissioned us to make disciples of all people groups. We are to do this under His absolute authority and with reliance upon His abiding presence. Through the ministry of the Apostle Paul as recorded by Luke in the Book of Acts, He has delivered to us a divinely authorized and approved strategy for fulfilling the Great Commission throughout the world of the Gentiles.

Q12. Having reflected deeply upon the contents of this Session, how do you plan to contribute to the expansion of Christ's kingdom through making disciples and establishing churches? Explain your answer.

Notes & Reflections

Session 5. Implications of Christ's Kingly Authority

The Problem of Spiritual Conflict

If Jesus Christ is King indeed, why is there still such intense spiritual conflict? Although He is enthroned, a spiritual battle is still raging, and it will continue to rage until the end. What we observe in the spiritual domain is similar to what can happen when a new leader becomes commander in chief. His army must still put down rebellions and insurrections that oppose his authority. Though the king is much more powerful than his adversaries, and the outcome is certain, nevertheless battles must still be waged and won before complete peace can be achieved. Even so, Jesus will continue reigning from His heavenly throne until He puts all his enemies under His feet.

Jesus the Conqueror

Consider the following passages which represent the current state of affairs and Christ's ultimate triumph:

1 Corinthians 15:25-28. For He must reign until He puts all His enemies under His feet. The last enemy to be abolished is death. For God has put everything under His feet. But when it says "everything" is put under Him, it is obvious that He who puts everything under Him is the exception. And when everything is subject to Christ, then the Son Himself will also be subject to the One who subjected everything to Him, so that God may be all in all.

Hebrews 2:7-9. You made him (mankind) lower than the angels for a short time; You crowned him with glory and honor and subjected everything under his feet. For in subjecting everything to him, He left nothing that is not subject to him. As it is, we do not yet see everything subjected to him. But we do see Jesus – made lower than the angels for a short time so that by God's grace He might taste Page 41 death for everyone – crowned with glory and honor because of His suffering in death.

Hebrews 2:14-15. Now since the children have flesh and blood in common, Jesus also shared in these, so that through His death He might destroy the one holding the power of death – that is, the Devil – and free those who were held in slavery all their lives by the fear of death.

Revelation 20:14. Death and Hades were thrown into the lake of fire. This is the second death, the lake of fire.

Q1. What do these passages teach us about the spiritual conflict that rages around us and its ultimate outcome?

Q2. When will everything be in subjection to Christ?

In the 2nd chapter of Hebrews, the writer makes clear that while Jesus' kingship is firmly established, the fullness of His reign has not yet been actualized. Now we see Him crowned with glory and honor on account of His death and resurrection, but we do not yet see all things under his feet. Although the cosmic death-blow to death and the powers of darkness has been dealt, it will not be realized in its fullness until Satan is cast into the lake of fire.

This brings us again to our place, as Christ's loyal subjects. We are called upon to participate in the process of bringing all things under the feet of our most worthy King. We begin by bringing our own attitudes, thoughts, emotions, words, and behaviors under His rule. We then extend His rule to others by offering them the good news of the gospel – the news of a sovereign, loving, and merciful King who has purchased our salvation at such a horrendous cost. To the extent that we are able, we should strive to see His rule expressed in our homes, through our government and its laws, in our educational systems, and in our Page 42 marketplaces. Everywhere

His people go as His ambassadors, they become change-agents for the Kingdom, enlarging the sphere of His rule until He comes again.

Q3. Reflect on the reality of a cosmic spiritual kingdom over which Christ rules as triumphant King, who is progressively putting His enemies under His feet. How does this impact your understanding of the gospel?

Q4. How will it affect the way you share the gospel?

Q5. How will it affect the way you train new disciples to walk in the way of Christ and the apostles?

Responding to Christ's Kingly Authority

Our humble response to King Jesus is to bow before Him in worship and adoration, praising Him in the words of Handel's glorious Messiah:

"Hallelujah! For the Lord God omnipotent reigneth... the kingdoms of this world are become the kingdoms of our Lord, and of His Christ; and He shall reign forever and ever... King of kings and Lord of lords... Worthy is the Lamb that was slain to receive power, and riches, and wisdom, and strength, and honor, and glory, and blessing... Blessing, and honor, glory and power, be unto Him that sitteth upon the throne, and unto the Lamb forever and ever... Amen!"

[Adapted from passages in Revelation, King James Version]

Q6. Highlight or list all the reasons given above to worship Jesus. Meditate on them and worship Him.

Q7. In addition to praise and adoration, how should we respond to the King?

Notes & Reflections

Session 6. Review & Discussion

The gospel of the kingdom of God is frequently overlooked in the preaching and teaching of the Christian gospel. In fact, since the first half of the 19th century, the preaching and teaching of the Christian gospel has emphasized the gospel of God and its promise of deliverance from bondage to evil, sin, and death. As a result, the way in which the gospel of the kingdom of God confronts human prideful rebellion against the righteous rule of God, and its demand for repentance and obedience, has been largely overlooked.

From our study thus far, it is clear that God conferred upon Jesus Christ His Son absolute, sovereign authority over the entire universe. The scope of His kingdom was predicted by the prophet Daniel. His kingdom is characterized by righteousness, justice, truth, and grace. Jesus' authority was prophesied by David in the 2nd Psalm, and it was confirmed by God the Father at Jesus' baptism and later at His transfiguration. He alone, as Son of God, is qualified to rule. His coronation was held in glory when, after His resurrection, He ascended to heaven to sit at the right hand of the Father. At that time He was given the name that is above every name – Yahweh, the Great I AM.

One day in the millennial kingdom, Jesus' rule will include the dimensions of political governance and a geographic domain. But now His kingdom is a spiritual and moral one; He rules through the hearts and lives of His loyal followers. The inception and in-breaking of His kingdom is recorded in the book of Acts, and it has become a worldwide movement over the past 2,000 years.

Only the righteous have a part in Jesus' kingdom. Indeed, the essence of sin is prideful rebellion against the rule of God. Therefore the proper response to the gospel of the kingdom of God is to repent and turn from our prideful rebellion and submit to the righteous, holy rule of Christ, the King.

Our responsibility as Kingdom citizens is to expand His kingdom by making disciples, establishing churches, and participating in waves of kingdom expansion by following the example of the Apostle Paul. Page 45 As His loyal subjects, we are to participate in the process of bringing all things under His feet, beginning with our own attitudes, thoughts, emotions, and behaviors. We are then to participate in His kingdom expansion as change-agents for the Kingdom – His ambassadors – sharing the good news of a sovereign, loving, and merciful King.

The call of the King is to a lifestyle of radical obedience.

Discussion Questions

Q1. Having completed this study guide, identify any misunderstandings or false expectations you may have had regarding the nature and character of the kingdom of God, the meaning of being a Christian, or the benefits of kingdom citizenship.

Q2. Discuss your willingness and the willingness of the people in your church community to submit to the laws of the kingdom of God with a radical lifestyle change. Page 46

Q3. Discuss the effectiveness of your church and its members in fulfilling the Great Commission, including Jesus' command to "teach them to obey everything I have commanded." Where might there be room for improvement?

Q4. How well does your church community practice the strategy for kingdom expansion pioneered by the Apostle Paul and discussed in Session 4? How well do the churches in your region of the world practice this pattern and method for expanding the kingdom of God?

Q5. How has the teaching in this study guide enhanced your love and appreciation for Jesus Christ as King, and your position as a citizen of His kingdom?

Q6. In your own words, analyze and discuss the connection between the kingship of Jesus Christ and saving faith.

Q7. What is the affirmation of Scripture concerning a person who professes to trust Jesus Christ as Savior, but who never truly submits to the rule of Christ as Lord and King? List as many passages as you can, and then select the three most relevant and telling passages in regard to this question. Reading each of the selected passages in context, discuss the meaning which you believe the author intended to convey.

Q8. Considering the Apostle John's testimony in the Book of Revelation, discuss the focus of eternal adoration and worship in regard to the person and work of Jesus Christ.

Notes & Reflections

Afterword

About Us

WitW is a product of Daystar Institute of Biblical Theology and Leadership
Development (DI), which is dedicated to
supporting local churches in fulfillment of their
mission of making disciples of all nations. We
have two offices: DI / NM is based in
Albuquerque, New Mexico, and DI / A is based
in Kampala, Uganda. Please do not hesitate to
contact us at www.DaystarInstitute/NM.us if
you have any questions or comments or wish to
request training in the use of our materials.

Peter Briggs is founder and president-emeritus of Daystar Institute of Biblical
Theology & Leadership Development. In addition to teaching and mentoring,
Dr. Briggs has authored the WitW Study Guide Series to challenge students in
uncompromising discipleship, practical Christian theology, and building a
biblical worldview. The WitW study has had a great impact in both East Africa
and the USA and is an excellent tool for encouraging and equipping disciples
of Jesus to actually live out their faith.

Dedication

The *Walking in the Way of Christ & the Apostles Study Guide Series* is dedicated
to Reverend Morris Wanje, whose prayers for God to raise up a means for
strengthening and equipping young pastors and church leaders in East Africa
caused the Holy Spirit of God to move upon the hearts of godly men and
women at Daystar Institute/NM to create this study.

Acknowledgments

I am grateful for the heroic efforts of our team of contributors, editors, board of directors, and all who have had a part in the development of the WitW study. In particular, I extend my heartfelt gratitude to my wife, Rosemarie, our daughter, Ruthanne Hamrick, and ministry associates John & Marcie Kinzer, Stephen Patterson, and Michael & Antoninah Mutinda, for their valuable input and help with the Study Guide Series; and to Darienne Dumas and Emily Fuller for proof-reading the texts.

Testimonials

"The *Walking in the Way of Christ & the Apostles* (WitW) series by Dr. Peter Briggs is a powerful tool for fulfilling Jesus' universal mandate to make disciples. WitW is theologically sound, conceptually brilliant, and life- changing for those who are trained by it. The impact of WitW is not only personal transformation into the image of Christ, but also a profound influence on families, churches, and the larger culture, whether in America or Africa or anywhere else. Peter Briggs is a theologian of substantial import, but he has not merely plied his theological craft in the halls of academia. With God's enablement, he has managed to translate biblical truth and disciple-making principles into something that actually works in the real world! Those who embrace and employ *Walking in the Way* in their own lives will find themselves part of a movement affecting generations to come."

Steven Collins, PhD, Executive Dean, Trinity Southwest University

"*Walking in the Way of Christ & the Apostles* (WitW) is a magnificent literary work in biblical theology that offers the student an education in practical Christianity. The WitW study was first introduced in November 2011; since that time we have been using it to instruct ministry leaders and rural pastors at a low cost, and the transformation of lives is phenomenal. Learners get to understand the message of the Bible and are able to study it effectively. In my own interaction with the material since 2012, I have come to realize that Jesus Christ is using it to revive His remnant in Kenya and other parts of Africa, teaching us how to think in a biblical way and be successful in all spheres of life. I am convinced that the WitW material holds the key to Africa's revival, and, in Yahweh's hand, it is a mighty tool for returning the continent back to Him."

Michael Mutinda, Team Leader, Daystar Institute / Africa

Walking in the Way of Christ & the Apostles
Study Guide Series

Part 1: Foundational Principles. These principles are foundational to equip the Christ-follower to have and to be governed by the mind of Christ.

1. The Way of God
2. The Storyline of the Bible
3. Biblical Reality
4. Discovering the Meaning of Scripture
5. Torah: The Fountainhead of Wisdom
6. The Two-Part Christian Gospel

Part 2: The Gospel of the Kingdom of God. Here we explore the ways in which the Christian gospel confronts the prideful rebellion of the human heart and exalts Christ as King over all.

7. Authority of the King
8. Called by the King
9. The Meaning of Discipleship
10. Disciplines of the Kingdom
11. Household of the King
12. The Second Coming of the King

Part 3 – The Gospel of God. This final set explores how the Christian gospel affords a complete solution to human depravity and the threefold problem of sin and death.

13. Introduction to the Gospel of God
14. The Reason for the Gospel of God
15. Content of the Gospel of God
16. Perversions of the Gospel of God
17. Application of the Gospel of God

Theological Readers (TR)

TR1 – Part 1: Foundational Principles
TR2 – Part 2: The Gospel of the Kingdom of God
TR3 – Part 3: The Gospel of God
TR4 – Resources and Appendices

Theological Handbooks (TH)

TH1 – Part 1: The Way of God
TH2 – Part 2
TH3 – Part 3

Connect with us at www.DaystarInstituteNM.us, or
Contact us via email at WalkingintheWayUSA@gmail.com

WitW
Walking in the Way of
Christ & the Apostles

www.ingramcontent.com/pod-product-compliance
Lightning Source LLC
Chambersburg PA
CBHW071933020426

42331CB00010B/2851